How to Resolve Your IRS Tax Debt Problems

How to Resolve Your IRS Tax Debt Problems

"ANYONE CONTEMPLATING SELF-REPRESENTATION BEFORE THE INTERNAL REVENUE SERVICE MUST READ THIS BOOK FIRST!"
LAWRENCE M. LAWLER

First Edition

Frank Haarlander, CPA, MBA, MS-Tax

F. Bryan Haarlander, EA

ISBN: 1540773493
ISBN 13: 9781540773494

DISCLAIMERS

This book is designed to provide educational information regarding the subject matters covered. While all attempts have been made to verify information provided in this book, the authors do not assume any responsibility for errors, inaccuracies, or omissions. Any perceived slights of people or organizations are unintentional.

This book is written with the understanding that the authors are not engaged in rendering legal, tax, accounting, financial, investment or any other advice related to your individual situation by publishing this book. Laws change rapidly, and you want to make sure when you implement a plan that it is based on the most current information available.

To avoid having to worry about which gender tense to use, we assumed that the taxpayer owing money to the IRS is a male.

Before implementing any of the tax resolution solutions discussed in this book, the authors recommend that you first consult with a competent and experienced tax resolution specialist to discuss your personal situation.

ABOUT THE AUTHORS

Frank Haarlander is a CPA (Certified Public Accountant) who has over forty years of experience working with business and individual clients. He earned his undergraduate degree in business administration from Rutgers College in New Brunswick, NJ. He earned his MBA at the Rutgers Professional School of Accounting in Newark, NJ, one of the country's best.

Frank started his business career with Lybrand, Ross Brothers & Montgomery in Philadelphia. The firm changed its name shortly afterwards to Coopers & Lybrand (C&L). Today, that firm is known as PricewaterhouseCoopers, LLP. During his six years there, he counseled individuals and businesses as to how to reduce their taxes and represented these individuals during IRS and state audits.

After leaving public accounting, for the following 22 years Frank held the position of Director of Taxes or Vice President of Taxes for some of this country's largest companies. He was very successful in implementing advanced tax-savings strategies and negotiating settlements with the IRS and state auditors.

During his years working for these companies, he earned a Masters in Tax degree from the Schools of Law and Commerce at Villanova University.

Along with his son Bryan, Frank founded a tax and accounting practice in 2001. Frank is a member of the Pennsylvania Institute of CPAs (PICPA), American Society of Tax Problem Solvers (ASTPS), and the National Society of Accountants (NSA).

Frank is a former member of the American Institute of CPAs (AICPA). He has held various executive positions and has served on the Board of Directors of the Philadelphia Chapter of the Tax Executives Institute. He has also served as an adjunct instructor at undergraduate accounting and graduate tax programs at local Philadelphia colleges and universities; and he speaks before the Chamber of Commerce, SCORE (a division of the U.S. Small Business Administration), and other business associations on various tax and business topics.

Frank received the 2016 Top Tax Practitioner award by the American Society of Tax Problem Solvers at its annual spring conference.

F. Bryan Haarlander is a co-founder of Keystone Financial Solutions, P.C. He has been providing tax and accounting services to business owners and individuals since 2001. Bryan is an Enrolled Agent who is licensed by the Internal Revenue Service to represent taxpayers before the IRS.

Bryan earned his bachelor's degree in Hotel and Restaurant Management from Penn State University. He began his business career in the hospitality industry. He has held various positions in the restaurant industry, ranging from working with family-owned businesses to managing the operations of national chains. Because of his vast experience and expertise in the hospitality industry, he works closely with restaurant and bar owner clients.

Before co-founding our CPA firm, Bryan started and managed an office for one of the major national tax preparation companies. Bryan's office later became one of the top-producing franchisees. During those years, he served as an instructor for tax preparers teaching them how to prepare personal income tax returns and was awarded certificates of accomplishment for his extensive knowledge of the Internal Revenue Code.

Bryan is a member of the American Society of Tax Problem Solvers (ASTPS) and the National Association of Tax Professionals (NATP).

ACKNOWLEDGEMENTS

We want to take this opportunity to thank the many people who have encouraged us to write this book, including clients and prospective clients who had tax problems and found the IRS world of rules and regulations extremely complex and confusing and were looking for a simple guide that explains their options.

We particularly want to thank Lawrence M. Lawler, CPA and Enrolled Agent, who is the National Director of the American Society of Tax Problem Solvers (ASTPS). ASTPS is a national non-profit professional association that was founded in 2003 to address the need for IRS tax problem resolution training and mentoring for over 1,000 professionals in the U.S.A. and Canada.

Larry teaches many of the educational programs offered by the ASTPS to train and educate tax professionals, like ourselves, who desire to become tax resolution specialists. His dedication to this tax specialty is without parallel. We cannot thank Larry enough for his mentoring over the years and for his valuable contributions to the writing of this book.

We also wish to thank L. G. Brooks, an Enrolled Agent, who is one of the ASTPS instructors and whose passion to assist taxpayers with tax problems is infectious to all of us who specialize in this field.

INTRODUCTION

Every taxpayer has the right to represent themselves before the IRS, including those who have been placed in collections by the IRS because of outstanding taxes due the IRS. We hope that this book will be of value to those taxpayers who decide to represent themselves as well as those who want a better understanding of the process before selecting a tax resolution specialist to represent them. This book was not meant to be all-inclusive, but rather a primer on some of the basics of the IRS Collections process.

In most cases, we do not recommend that taxpayers represent themselves before the IRS. Think of the adage that "An attorney who represents himself has a fool for a client." The tax law and IRS regulations are quite complex and a tax resolution specialist learns his craft over a period that spans many years. For someone to think that they can represent themselves is often a "penny wise, dollar foolish" approach. In those rare occurrences when we meet with a taxpayer who has a very simple case and we believe that they can handle the case, we provide them with the guidance they need to represent themselves.

Understanding the rules and procedures of the IRS to resolve IRS tax debt is quite complex. Many tax professionals do not understand how to resolve IRS tax debt problems because it is a specialty in the tax world and they feel more comfortable outsourcing this work to tax resolution specialists who understand the "ins and outs" of how the IRS works. They take this action because it is in the best interests of their clients and because they wish to remain compliant with IRS Circular 230,

§10.35. In that paragraph, the IRS requires that "A practitioner must possess the necessary competence to engage in practice before the Internal Revenue Service. Competent practice requires the appropriate level of knowledge, skill, thoroughness, and preparation necessary for the matter for which the practitioner is engaged." When interviewing firms to represent you before the IRS, it is imperative that you perform your due diligence. You want to make sure that the firm that is representing you understands your rights as a taxpayer, will not be intimidated by IRS personnel, and has a track record of successfully navigating the IRS maze of its Internal Revenue Manual (IRM) to resolve their clients' tax problems.

TABLE OF CONTENTS

CHAPTER 1

How Do Tax Problems Arise?

Millions of Americans are drowning in tax debt. If you find yourself in this situation, you need to know that you are not alone. Per the Internal Revenue Service (IRS) 2015 data book, there are over 13 million delinquent taxpayer accounts with over $137 billion of assessed taxes, interest and penalties due the IRS.

We realize that sometimes bad things happen to good people. There are often life-changing events in our lives that we cannot control. There are also events that we thought could be controlled, but unfortunately the devastating consequences of those events could not be foreseen and created havoc in our lives.

When these life-changing events occur, your daily priorities change and being in tax compliance is not always your principal focus or concern. Thus, you may fail to file your tax returns or fail to pay the taxes due. Let's look at a small sampling of these life-altering events.

- You can be in relatively good health and suddenly you find that your mental and physical skills are diminished. You may find it extremely difficult to concentrate on your financial affairs, including filing tax returns and paying the IRS the taxes you owe.
- A member of your immediate family dies unexpectedly. Not only do you grieve over the loss of a loved one, but the

deceased may have been the family member who took care of the filing of tax returns. It is not uncommon that when someone is facing a task which they do not feel comfortable doing, they are prone to put it off to another day. These tomorrows accumulate and eventually your tax responsibilities have been ignored for numerous months and possibly years.

- You have been paying your taxes and filing tax returns on time for 20+ years, only to come into the office one day to learn that your employment has been terminated. You did nothing to deserve this, but the company has decided to outsource your job overseas where the wages paid are considerably less than those paid in the U.S.A. Your employer's industry may be shrinking due to competition and senior management has decided that headcount must be reduced – and you are one of the unfortunate ones to receive a pink slip.

- You have been happily married for several years and now your spouse wants to divorce you. All the assets you have accumulated, your retirement benefits, and your current income may now be reduced by the divorce proceedings.

- You decided to go into business for yourself or you invested in a business opportunity that was going to make you rich. Things didn't work out as expected, and you find that a substantial part of your wealth that took you years or decades to accumulate has vanished overnight.

- The IRS decided to examine your return and the IRS auditor finds that you owe a substantial amount of money because you couldn't substantiate your tax deductions in accordance with IRS regulations and rules or you misinterpreted the tax law. Perhaps your spouse failed to report all his income, and you, the innocent spouse who stayed home to take care of your children, receive a significant assessment from the IRS for the simple reason that you filed a joint return with your husband that makes you liable for his taxes.

- Your employer failed to pay the IRS the payroll and income taxes that were due. The employer was having a "temporary" cash flow problem and someone decided that the cash flow problem could be corrected by not paying the IRS its payroll taxes for one tax period, and then to repay the IRS the following tax period. However, the "temporary" cash flow problem continued for several tax periods. As a bookkeeper for your employer, you helped process the company's payroll but had no management decisions. One day you receive a letter from the IRS saying that it considers you a responsible person for your company's payroll filings, and that you are responsible for paying the IRS 100% of the trust fund taxes due.

■ Some taxpayers owe the IRS because of what is called a "substitute for return" (SFR). The IRS receives information (Forms W-2s and Forms 1099) from various third parties. If the taxpayer fails to file a tax return with the IRS, the IRS computers will analyze if the IRS believes a refund is due the taxpayer or if there is a balance due the IRS. If there is an expected balance due the IRS, the IRS prepares a SFR. Now before you begin thinking that this is a great way to get free tax preparation services, you need to think again. When preparing these returns, the IRS only considers the income items, ignores all deductions except for providing the taxpayer with a single exemption and the standard deduction for a single taxpayer. The purpose of these returns is to maximize the amounts owed by the taxpayer to the IRS in the hope that this significant assessment will motivate the taxpayer to file the missing tax returns and pay the taxes due. For example, consider a day trader. The trader makes a multitude of trades each day, and it is not uncommon that the gross proceeds from these trades generate over a million dollars in gross revenues. If the IRS only considers the gross proceeds and ignores what the day trader paid to acquire the stock, you can imagine that the trader's federal tax liability will be grossly overstated by the IRS using its methodology.

■ Then there are the tax protestors. The IRS has no sympathy for these persons as they protest not paying their taxes based on arguments that our courts have found are without merit. Many believe that these people have brought their IRS tax problems on themselves.

CHAPTER 2

Why Is My Tax Liability So Much?

You realize that you owe the IRS for unpaid taxes. However, when you receive the IRS assessment notice, you are shocked when you see the balance due and don't understand why it is such a large amount.

There are two elements that significantly add up that are major contributors to the total IRS tax debt that you owe.

The first element is interest. As Albert Einstein is quoted, "Compound interest is the eighth wonder of the world. He who understands it, earns it . . . he who doesn't . . . pays it." The IRS clearly understands compound interest because they charge interest compounded daily. For taxpayers who file late or pay late, the rate changes monthly. The IRS uses the federal short-term rate (published monthly) plus 3%.

The second element is penalties that the IRS assesses. It has been stated that the IRS has over 100 different types of penalties. In this chapter, we are only focusing on two of those penalties. These penalties are (1) the failure to file a tax return and (2) the failure to pay the taxes due.

If you find yourself in a position where you have your return prepared but do not have the monies to pay the taxes due, do yourself a **BIG** favor and file the return and pay what you can afford to pay. This strategy will minimize the assessment of penalties.

If you owe tax and don't file on time, the IRS assesses you a penalty of 5% of the tax due for each month, or portion of a month, that the return is late. This penalty will be assessed for no more than a period of 5 months, which is equal to 25% of the taxes due. Let's assume that you requested an extension of time to file. Accordingly, rather than your Form 1040 tax return being due on April 15, you receive a 6-month automatic extension of time to file until October 15. Due to events beyond your control, you filed your return one day after the extended due date of October 15 (October 16) because you were expecting a sizable deposit to hit your bank account which would allow you to pay your taxes in full. Although in your mind your return was filed just 1 day late, the IRS late filing penalty will be 25% of the tax liability, because it is assessed at 5% per month or part of a month for filing late. The penalty is assessed from the original due date of April 15. Thus, the months of April, May, June, July, August, September, and October are late filing months. Fortunately, although your return was filed seven months (or portions thereof) late, the maximum penalty of 5% per month is assessed for only 5 months. If your return is over 60 days late, the minimum penalty for late filing is the smaller of $135 or 100 percent of the tax owed.

If you file on time but don't pay all amounts due on time, you'll generally have to pay a late payment penalty of one–half of one percent (0.5%) of the actual tax owed for each month, or part of a month, that the tax remains unpaid from the due date, until the tax is paid in full. The maximum limit to the failure-to-pay penalty is 25%. As you can see, the failure to file penalty of 5% is 10 times greater than the failure to pay penalty of 0.5%, which is why it is important to file a tax return on time even if you do not have the funds to pay the tax.

Using the fact pattern discussed above, let's assume the taxpayer files an extension of time to file Form 1040 until October 15. The filing of Form 4868 (the request for an extension of time to file) does not extend the time to pay the tax due. Thus, regardless of the date when a late tax payment is made, the penalty for failure to pay begins from the original due date of the return, April 15 (and not the extended due, October 15 in this example).

If both the failure to file and failure to pay penalties are applicable for the same month, the taxpayer pays a penalty of 4.5% for that month (the 5% late filing penalty less 0.5% late payment penalty).

While it would appear that if a taxpayer fails to timely file and pay would pay a combined penalty of 50% (25% max for failure to file and 25% max for failure to pay), the actual combined rate charged by the IRS is 47.5% (22.5% late filing and 25% late payment).

So why do you owe such a large amount? Your IRS tax debt may have increased by 47.5% because of penalties and in addition, the IRS charges interest compounded daily.

CHAPTER 3

Understanding the Statute of Limitations

A statute of limitation (SOL) is the time period established by the Internal Revenue Code (IRC) to review, analyze and resolve tax related issues. The IRC requires that the IRS assess, refund, credit and collect taxes within a specified time period, otherwise these actions are prohibited.

The IRS is required to assess (income tax, penalties, and interest) within 3 years after date of filing. The SOL begins to run *the day after* a return is considered filed.

Taxpayers must file their refund claims within 3 years from the date of filing, or within 2 years from the date the tax was paid. This is why tax professionals recommend that tax returns be mailed to the IRS via U.S.P.S. certified mailing or by e-filing so that the date of filing can be verified and substantiated.

The IRS has a 6-year SOL to assess taxes if the taxpayer omits or understates greater than 25% of his gross income reported on his return. This provision also includes an understatement of gross income by reason of an overstatement of uncovered cost or other basis.

If the SOL is about to expire, the IRS may request that the taxpayer enter into a written agreement to consent to extend the SOL. The taxpayer is not required to extend the SOL and the IRS is required to notify the taxpayer of his right to refuse to extend the SOL. However, in certain cases it may be to the taxpayer's benefit to agree to extend the SOL. Such a case may be when the IRS is willing to concede one issue in return for the taxpayer agreeing to extend the SOL on another issue.

If a taxpayer files an amended return, it does not extend the statute for assessment. However, when a taxpayer files an amended return within 60 days of the SOL expiring, the IRS is allowed an additional 60 days to assess. The "extra 60 days" is tacked onto the date that the SOL would have expired.

If the taxpayer files a false or fraudulent return with the intent to evade tax, the taxpayer attempts to willfully defeat or evade tax, or the taxpayer fails to file a return, there is no SOL. In these cases, the SOL never closes and the IRS can assess the taxpayer indefinitely.

Since the date a return is filed is relevant to the SOL, to have a return considered as being filed the return must contain sufficient data, the filing must purport to be a "return", there must be an honest attempt to satisfy the law, and the return must be signed under penalty of perjury.

When a taxpayer fails to file his return, as previously stated, the IRS may file a "Substitute for Return" (SFR). The SFR results in an assessment of tax and the collection SOL starts. Hence, it is generally advisable to file a tax return if for no other reason than to start the running of the SOL.

When a tax has been assessed within the period of the SOL, such tax may be collected by levy or by court proceeding if such action is taken within 10 years after the assessment of the tax. In other words, the IRS has 10 years to collect an assessed tax. There can be no collection of taxes without taxes being assessed. The 10-year period is determined from the *day after the tax is assessed*, not from the date of filing. This 10-year SOL is referred to as the CSED, the Collection Statute Expiration Date.

There are provisions in the IRC that suspend the 10-year collection SOL. Examples of such items include, but are not limited to, absence from the country for 6 months or more, filing of IRS Form 911, bankruptcy filing, request for a collection due process (CDP) hearing, offer-in-compromise (OIC) request, and the issuance of a statutory notice of deficiency by the IRS. When deciding the best alternative to resolving IRS tax debts, it is imperative that the CSED be analyzed and computed considering all the provisions that suspend the 10-year statute.

When dealing with the IRS to resolve tax debt, an experienced tax resolution specialist will consider the impact any contemplated tax resolution solution will have on the statute of limitations. In some cases, it may make sense not to take certain resolution action, such as filing for an Offer-In-Compromise, because the taxpayer could be in a better position if the SOL were allowed to expire.

CHAPTER 4

IRS Collection Process – An Overview

The IRS Collection Process, in its most simplistic form, is as follows:

- An Income Tax Return is Filed or a Substitute for Return (SFR) is prepared by the IRS
- IRS Assesses Tax
- 10-year Collection Statute of Limitations *starts day after tax is assessed*
- IRS sends billing notices to the taxpayer
- Notice of Federal Tax Lien is Filed on Taxpayer's Property (liens are discussed in Chapter 5)
- IRS Sends Notice of Intent to Levy (levies are discussed in Chapter 5)
- IRS Sends Final Notice of Intent to Levy and Notifies Taxpayer of Right to a Hearing
- Appeals: Collection Due Process, Equivalent Hearing, and Collection Appeal Procedure
- Payments Are Made by the Taxpayer

In the earlier chapters, we discussed what constitutes the filing of a return, the IRS assessing the tax, and when the 10-year Statute of Limitations on Collection begins.

Usually over a 15-week period, the IRS has a host of notices it sends to taxpayers to collect past due taxes. These include CP14 which is a balance due notice and CP501 which is an important notice about an unpaid balance. The notices notify the taxpayer of unpaid taxes for a specific tax year and the amount that is due the IRS. Approximately 5 weeks later, these notices are followed up with a CP503 which reminds the taxpayer that the IRS has not heard from him and he still has an unpaid balance due the IRS. The CP504 notice is then sent reminding the taxpayer that there is a balance due. It also informs the taxpayer that if the balance due is not paid immediately, the IRS will seize (levy) the taxpayer's state income tax refund and apply it to pay the amount he owes. The CP504B notice is similar to the CP504 notice, but it is broader in that the IRS states that it will seize (levy) certain property or rights to property and apply the proceeds to the amount that is owed to the IRS. When comparing these notices, the IRS language becomes more threatening with each succeeding notice.

Taxpayers have a tendency to ignore payment notices and warning of the filing of a federal tax lien. The IRS notifies a delinquent taxpayer that it may file a Notice of Federal Tax Lien (IRS Form 668-Y) at any time to protect its interest. A lien is a public notice filed with the appropriate county or state office alerting creditors that the government has a right to your assets. Federal tax liens are automatic and statutory in all cases, even without the 668-Y filing. The IRS is required to advise the taxpayer of the lien filing five (5) days *after* filing a federal tax lien. Consequently, the IRS has already filed its lien when you receive the lien notice.

Those taxpayers who have continuously ignored the IRS notices demanding payment and the filing of a federal tax lien often seek help when the IRS notifies them of its intent to levy (seize the taxpayer's assets). The IRS sends the taxpayer a Letter 1058, CP90, LT 11, or CP297 notice, "Final Notice – Notice of Intent to Levy and Notice of Your Right to a Hearing".

When the IRS is going to levy a taxpayer's assets, the IRS notifies the taxpayer *prior* to levy action giving the taxpayer an opportunity to request a hearing before IRS takes possession of their property.

Upon receipt of this Final Notice, you have 30 days from the date of the notice to request a Collection Due Process (CDP) Appeal hearing which requires the filing of IRS Form 12153, enter into an installment agreement to pay your tax debt, or propose an Offer-in-Compromise. Failure to pay the balance due, make payment arrangements, or request a hearing within the 30-day period, the IRS has the right to take your property, or rights to your property. Property includes real estate, vehicles, business assets, bank accounts, wages, commissions, social security benefits, retirement income, and other income.

During this 30-day window and while the CDP appeal is being considered by the Appeals office (should the taxpayer timely file Form 12153), all collection actions are halted by the IRS (unless new tax liabilities are generated by the taxpayer). The IRS Appeals Office prefers that the hearing be held by phone, though a face-to-face meeting can be requested. The IRS has the final decision as to whether it will be a telephone or face-to-face hearing.

Unfortunately, too many taxpayers wait until they receive this Final Notice before asking for help from a tax resolution specialist. Procrastination can result in the taxpayer losing certain appeal rights. For example, if the 30-day CDP window is missed, the taxpayer can request an Equivalent Hearing if filed within one year of the date on the Final Notice.

Unlike a CDP hearing where collection efforts are halted and the taxpayer has the right to take its appeal to the U. S. Tax Court should Appeals not rule in favor of the taxpayer, there is no requirement that the IRS cease collection activity (e.g., levy action) when an equivalent hearing is granted and the taxpayer has no right to a judicial review in Tax Court.

Whenever a lien or levy is issued by the IRS, the taxpayer has the right to request a Collection Appeal Process (CAP) hearing. This is a procedural review to make sure the IRS Collections Division has followed IRS procedures. It does allow a taxpayer to get his case in front of an Appeals Officer and halts collection efforts by the IRS.

CHAPTER 5

Liens & Levies

A lien arises whenever a demand for payment is made by the IRS and the taxpayer fails to pay. The IRS need not notify the taxpayer in advance of the filing of a lien. Tax resolution specialists often refer to this as "the silent lien" as it automatically exists upon assessment. The IRS may file a Notice of Federal Tax Lien. The IRS files this notice to inform third-party creditors of the IRS lien on the taxpayer's assets to protect the IRS's interest in the property.

The lien attaches to all property currently owned and all property acquired after the lien is filed.

A levy is when the IRS seizes (takes) the taxpayer's property. The IRS uses a levy to get the taxpayer's attention when the taxpayer has failed to respond to IRS requests or failed to provide the collection division with information it requested.

There are two types of levies, a regular and a continuing levy.

A regular levy seizes whatever the taxpayer owns at that particular moment. For example, the IRS may levy against the taxpayer's bank account. When the bank receives the IRS levy notice, the bank is required to set aside the funds in the bank account *on that date* and send those funds to the IRS in 21 days. For example, taxpayer A has $8.30 in his account on the date when the IRS levies his bank account. On the following day, the taxpayer's paycheck for $3,000 is automatically deposited into his checking account. The bank will send the IRS $8.30 in 21 days, and not $3,008.30, as the $8.30 was the amount in the account on the date the levy was received by the bank.

A continuous levy remains in effect until it is released by the IRS. An example of this type of levy is when the IRS garnishes a taxpayer's wages. Until the tax debt is satisfied or other arrangements are made with the IRS, the taxpayer's wages will be garnished every pay period until the tax debt is satisfied. The IRS allows the taxpayer a standard deduction and personal exemptions. Everything above this exempt amount will be sent to the IRS by the employer.

Levies usually catch the attention of the taxpayer and that is when they decide it is time to get professional help. Whereas the taxpayer ignored the IRS for several months to reach this point, he now has religion and wants the levy to disappear immediately. To release a levy, the IRS will want all missing tax returns to be filed, the IRS collection forms to be completed, and supporting documentation submitted to substantiate the taxpayer's claimed expenses.

CHAPTER 6

Resolving IRS Tax Debt

The five most commonly used alternatives to resolve IRS tax debt (taxes, interest and penalties) are:

- Installment Agreements
- Offers-in-Compromise
- Currently-Not-Collectible Status
- Bankruptcy
- Abatement of Penalties

While the IRS will do everything in its power to collect the tax (and interest and penalties) you owe, there are reasons why the IRS may be willing to reach a mutually satisfying payment arrangement with you that may even include forgiving part of your tax debt.

The decision as to which option is the best option for you depends entirely upon your unique facts and circumstances. A tax resolution specialist will consider each of these options, their pros and cons, your age, your level of education, your income and expenses, the liquidity of your assets, and how much time is left on the Statute of Limitations.

These methods of resolving IRS tax debt are discussed in more detail in the chapters to follow.

CHAPTER 7

Installment Agreements

If a taxpayer is unable to pay his tax debt immediately, the IRS allows the taxpayer to make monthly payments through an installment agreement. As with any tax resolution option, there are pros and cons associated with setting up an installment plan.

What are the benefits (pros) to the taxpayer of entering into an installment agreement?

- IRS ceases collection activity while the request is being reviewed.
- If the installment agreement is accepted, IRS collection efforts are suspended as long as the terms of the agreement are being followed.
- It may be possible to have a lien or levy removed under certain circumstances.
- It may be the easiest arrangement for the IRS to approve.
- If you are in a seasonal business, the IRS may be willing to make seasonal adjustments to the monthly amount you are required to remit.
- You may wind up never paying the full tax debt due the IRS.
- Any refunds you may generate in future years will automatically be applied by the IRS to your tax debt until it is paid in full.

What are the cons to the taxpayer of entering into an installment agreement?

- User fees are paid to enter into such an agreement
- Financial disclosure may be required (dependent upon type of installment agreement and amount owed)
- Penalties and interest continue to accrue
- May have to keep paying beyond the original CSED (see partial installment agreements)

Depending upon how much you owe the IRS, there are various types of installment agreements. To be eligible for an installment agreement, you must have filed all required tax returns.

Statutory Installment Agreement is when a taxpayer owes $10,000 or less of tax and the debt can be paid off within 36 months. This is an arrangement most taxpayers can handle themselves by calling the IRS Collections Division telephone number found on the IRS website, www.irs.gov.

Streamlined Installment Agreement rules changed in September 2016 under a test program being run by the IRS. If you qualify for this program, you need not provide the detailed financial information found on IRS Form 433-A to the IRS. The test program allows taxpayers who have filed all required income tax returns and who owe $100,000 or less (including interest and penalties) to pay off their IRS tax debt over 84 months providing that the Collection Statute Expiration Dates (CSED) don't expire before or during that time period. If CSEDs will be expiring, the amount must be paid over the life of the CSED or you must provide financials. The installment payment must be made using a direct debit from the taxpayer's bank account (IRS Form 433D) or from the taxpayer's wages every month (IRS Form 2159).

Regular (Standard) Installment Agreement is applicable when the total assessed balance is less than $250,000 or you do not qualify for the previously discussed installment agreements. If your balance due is over $250,000, you will be dealing with a Revenue Officer who is a highly trained and experienced IRS employee. These agreements require the submission of financial information which could require IRS Forms 433-A, 433-B and/or 433-F. The financials will be used by the IRS to determine the monthly amount the taxpayer can pay. When completing these forms, the IRS considers all sources of gross income and not all monthly expenses will be considered by the IRS. The IRS uses established national or local standards as to what expenses can be claimed by the taxpayer and the amounts allowable to compute the taxpayer's ability to pay.

Partial-Pay Installment Agreement (PPIA) is not limited by the dollar amount of the taxpayer's tax debt. These agreements require the submission of financial information which could require IRS Forms 433-A, 433-B and/or 433-F and the appropriate form(s) are required to be re-submitted biennially. The IRS only allows what it considers to be necessary expenses in computing the taxpayer's ability to pay. If the IRS believes that the taxpayer will acquire an asset after the CSED, the IRS may require that the collection statute be extended (up to five years) to enter in this type of agreement. The IRS can only secure this waiver when entering into a PPIA and not after the PPIA has been accepted. The IRS is allowed to file liens during the payment period to protect its interests. If the taxpayer owns assets, the IRS almost always requests that the assets be disposed to pay down the IRS tax debt. Note that the extended Statute of Limitations on Collection also allows IRS to collect more of the liability albeit at the reduced monthly payment.

Regardless of the type of installment agreed that is used, if the taxpayer defaults on his agreement, the installment agreement is nullified and the taxpayer is back into collections. Common mistakes taxpayers make when entering into an installment agreement with the IRS include:

- Agreeing to pay more each month than the taxpayer can comfortably afford to pay.
- Believing that the postmark date determines the payment date. Unfortunately for installment agreements, the IRS uses the date received, not the postmarked date. It is best to remit payment by mail at least 10 days prior to the installment payment due date for the IRS to timely process your payment and have it recorded in your tax account or to make your installment payments by direct debit from your checking account.
- Failing to stay in compliance with the IRS. All subsequent tax return filings must be timely made (including extensions), W-2 withholdings must be adequate for the current tax year, and if self-employed, estimated taxes must be remitted.

CHAPTER 8

Offer in Compromise

Whenever you hear the phrase "pennies on the dollar" in relation to federal tax liabilities, you are hearing a reference to the Offer-in-Compromise (OIC) program. Unfortunately, this phrase was and may still be used by unscrupulous tax resolution firms to mislead taxpayers into thinking that they qualify for this program and that the IRS will accept *any* offer to pay less than the full amount due the IRS. These "OIC mills" lure in desperate and frightened delinquent taxpayers with false assurances that their tax problems will be resolved . . . after collecting a substantial fee for their services. In some cases, these OIC mills take little or no action and eventually the taxpayer learns that their IRS debt has actually increased due to accumulating penalties and interest. If you are contemplating using a firm you learned about on the radio or cable TV, take the time to Google "Roni Deutch", "TaxMasters", and "J. K. Harris". These were three very large tax resolution firms who were closed by their state's attorney general offices for consumer fraud or some other crime. Researching the credibility of the firm you plan to use is very important. You do not want to add to your tax problems and create more anxiety for yourself by working with a disreputable firm.

There are three types of OIC filings. These are:

- Doubt as to liability
- Doubt as to collectability
- Effective Tax Administration/Special Circumstances

Since the doubt as to collectability is the most prominent of the three, this chapter will solely focus on it.

The OIC program is intended to give taxpayers without the financial means to pay their tax debt a way to pay what they can afford to pay, and then start over. The best OIC candidates are taxpayers that have very little in the way of assets, no remaining income after IRS allowable expenses are considered, have their best earning years behind them, and tend to be underemployed or unemployed.

While the OIC program is the most familiar tax resolution alternative known to taxpayers, to the surprise of many it is the least frequently applicable resolution strategy for a federal tax debt. The most successful resolution strategies are the previously discussed installment agreements.

OICs comprise less than one percent of closed collection cases. IRS statistics show that approximately 60% of OICs are rejected by the IRS. The high rejection rate is likely a result of the numerous offers submitted by taxpayers and/or practitioners lacking knowledge of the system and the skills to apply effective planning. Similar to the installment agreement requirements, to be considered for an OIC, the taxpayer must:

- Have filed all past due tax returns;
- Not currently be incurring new tax liabilities;
- Agree to properly file and pay on all tax returns, on time, for the next 5 years; and
- Agree to let the IRS keep any tax refunds due the taxpayer through the year in which the OIC is accepted.

Failure to abide by these rules will result in rejection of the offer, or default of the offer agreement and result in full reinstatement of all (remaining) tax liabilities that had been eliminated.

An OIC is submitted using IRS Form 656. It requires the completion of IRS Form 433-A(OIC) for an individual taxpayer along with *complete* supporting documentation (generally for the most recent three months). The 433-A(OIC) form is designed to compute the Reasonable Collection Potential (RCP), the amount that the IRS determines as an acceptable offer.

In its simplest form, RCP is the sum of two factors. The first factor is the realizable net worth (fair market value of assets less liabilities). This is often the easiest part to satisfy as many taxpayers, due to their adverse financial situation, have few assets with any realizable equity. For many taxpayers, their most valuable asset is their home, and many times the mortgage and home equity loans on the residence exceed the value of the home. Thus, they have no realizable equity in their home.

The second factor that is added to the realizable net worth is the taxpayer's remaining income for the next 12 or 24 months. In other words, the RCP (settlement amount) = (1) the net realizable equity in the taxpayer's assets plus (2) the monthly remaining income x (12 or 24). The 12 and 24 factors are discussed below. A mistake that some taxpayers make is assuming that because their *actual* monthly expenses exceed their monthly income, they have no disposable income. Unfortunately for the taxpayer, the IRS has its own standards that limit actual expenses. *The IRS has established national and local standards that it uses to determine allowable expenses to compute the amount of income left over each month to pay the IRS debt.* In addition, there are certain types of expenses that the IRS formula will exclude in its computation. Common disallowed expenses are college tuition payments for a dependent, private school tuition, charitable contributions, tithing, vacation home payments, and unsecured loan payments. Taxpayers are allowed to claim a portion of their state tax debt payments when payments are being made to a state and a state payment plan is in place. The amount of the state tax payment allowed is based using a pro-rata approach between IRS debt and state debt.

It can easily take the IRS between 6-12 months before it begins to review the submitted OIC. At that time, the taxpayer will be notified that the IRS is considering the offer, but the financial data submitted with the original application is not current and that the taxpayer needs to resubmit the OIC using current financial data. In essence, the taxpayer winds up submitting a second Form 433-A(OIC) with supporting documents. Once the IRS completes its review of the taxpayer's offer, often there are negotiations back and forth and the original offer amount may need to be increased to have the IRS accept the OIC.

It has been our experience that many in the IRS detest approving OICs and there is a very likely chance that the OIC will be rejected, including those that should be accepted per the IRS rules and guidelines. We have been told by former IRS employees that there are some in the IRS who believe that everyone should pay their fair share, and they have a bias towards OICs. When a bona fide OIC has been submitted and rejected by the OIC unit of the IRS, don't despair. It is time to go to the Appeals Office. Settlement officers have the authority to accept or reject an OIC based on their own findings, rather than the findings of the OIC examiner.

Since taxpayers have alternatives in deciding how to address their IRS tax debt, we believe that Form 433-A or 433-A (OIC) should be completed as a tool for helping the taxpayer determine his best resolution strategy. If you want to succeed against the IRS, you need to know what they know, and this includes knowing what the IRS expects to be able to collect from the taxpayer. If the taxpayer owes more than the RCP, he might be a good OIC candidate. If he owes less than RCP, he is most likely going to end up in an Installment Agreement. If RCP is less than zero, then he is a good Currently Not Collectible candidate (discussed in Chapter 9).

Because an acceptance of an OIC means the IRS is settling for less money than owed to it, the IRS scrutinizes the financial data submitted to it very carefully. One could say that the IRS assumes the taxpayer is not being fully truthful, and acts accordingly. The IRS goes through an extensive investigation to verify the information on Form 433-A(OIC). It looks for undisclosed assets the taxpayer may own and income that was omitted or understated. The IRS looks at various public records sources, including department of motor vehicles, census data, deeds, Uniform Commercial Code (UCC) filings, credit reports, e-Bay reports, just to name a few resources used by the IRS.

When an OIC is filed, the 10-year statute to collect the tax debt is extended day-for-day while an offer is in processing, plus 30 days if it is ultimately denied. Thus, there are times when the filing of an OIC can be detrimental to the taxpayer as discussed in Chapter 3.

There are two well-known payment options available with the submission of an OIC. The number of months over which the remaining income must be calculated into the offer amount is based on the payment plan option selected. For the lump sum cash offer, remaining income is multiplied by 12 months. For the periodic payment offer, remaining income is multiplied by 24 months.

If the taxpayer selects the lump sum payment option, the entire offer amount must be paid within five months of acceptance of the offer. A minimum non-refundable deposit of 20% of the offer amount must be submitted with the application unless the taxpayer meets low income qualifications. The taxpayer need not make any periodic payments while the offer is being processed. Using this option results in paying the smallest possible offer amount, because the taxpayer's remaining income under the RCP calculation formula is multiplied by a factor of 12 (rather than 24).

The second payment option, referred to as the periodic payment, requires the taxpayer to make regular payments on the OIC while the IRS is considering the offer. These payments are non-refundable, and the first payment must be included with the Offer application while the IRS is considering it, unless the taxpayer meets low income guidelines. The taxpayer must pay the full offer amount within 24 months. For SOL reasons, each payment on the memo line of a periodic check should designate the most recent tax period. In other words, have your payments applied against the taxes owed to the most recently filed tax years. If you do not designate the tax year, the IRS will apply your payment against the earliest years first as those are the years that the SOL will expire first. For example, if the taxpayer owes the IRS for tax years 2007 through 2014, the appropriate memo line would read "apply to 2014 Form 1040 only." If this step is not done, the IRS will apply the payment to the 2007 tax year.

When deciding between the lump-sum and periodic payment options, one needs to consider the taxpayer's financial condition to see if the 20% deposit is doable, and if the offer is going to take 12 months before a decision is rendered and since the payments under both options are non-refundable, which payment option works best for the household budget of the taxpayer. This is one area where working with an experienced tax resolution specialist can be very valuable. A resolution specialist understands how the IRS operates and can offer alternative payment options that are significantly more taxpayer friendly.

Keep in mind that penalties and interest continue to accrue on the tax liability while OIC payments are being made, even though ultimately those penalties and interest go away if the Offer is accepted. If the OIC is rejected by the IRS, then the taxpayer is responsible for not only the outstanding taxes, interest and penalties when the offer was submitted, but also the penalties and interest that accrued while the offer was being considered.

If the taxpayer's OIC is accepted by the IRS and the taxpayer later defaults on the terms of the OIC, the IRS will again begin to assess penalties and interest.

If you are considering filing an OIC on behalf of yourself, keep in mind that 60% of OICs are rejected and if the IRS denies the exclusion of certain assets or expenses, this is where having a tax resolution professional represent you can make a significant difference in the outcome of the Offer application. Based on our experience, using a tax resolution specialist will likely result in a reduced offer amount meaning that you are offering less money to the IRS to settle your entire tax debt. The specialist knows of acceptable strategies to maximize expenses that the IRS will accept and how to structure payment options to better fit the cash flow needs of the taxpayer. These dollar savings often exceed the representation fee. In addition, you have the peace of mind knowing that you are working with a specialist who is protecting your taxpayer rights and that you will not need to speak with the IRS.

CHAPTER 9

Currently Not Collectible

Currently not collectible (CNC) status provides the taxpayer with *temporary* relief from IRS collection activities. It is available to those taxpayers who are unable to pay *any* of the amount due the IRS because payment would prevent them from meeting their basic living expenses. In other words, the taxpayer would suffer economic hardship.

CNC status is a means to request that the IRS delay collection until the taxpayer can pay. If the IRS determines that the taxpayer cannot pay any of his tax debt because of financial hardship, the IRS assigns CNC status to the taxpayer's account until his financial condition improves.

Being CNC does not mean the debt goes away. It means the IRS has determined that the taxpayer cannot afford to pay the debt at that time. Penalties and interest will continue to accrue until the tax debt is paid in full or the 10-year SOL expires.

Prior to approving a request to delay collection, the IRS will ask the individual taxpayer to complete a Collection Information Statement (Form 433-A or 433-F) and provide supporting documentation to verify his financial status. We discussed in Chapter 8 how the Reasonable Collection Potential (RCP) is computed, and if the taxpayer's financial information shows that the RCP is less than zero, then the taxpayer is a good CNC candidate.

As stated above, CNC status is a temporary relief given to the taxpayer. It is not intended to be permanent. The IRS will monitor the taxpayer's sources of income as reported to the IRS by third parties, and the IRS will periodically request the re-submission of the 433 forms to analyze the taxpayer's current financial condition.

While the taxpayer is in CNC status, the IRS may temporarily suspend enforced collection actions, such as issuing a levy. However, it may still file a Notice of Federal Tax Lien to protect its interests.

The SOL continues to run while the taxpayer is in CNC status. Thus, it is possible for the 10 year collection statute to expire during the time that the taxpayer is classified as CNC.

CHAPTER 10

Penalty Abatement

Every tax professional has likely been asked this question by a client: "Will the IRS forgive my interest and penalties if I pay my taxes in full?"

The IRS does not have the ability to forgive interest since this is a statutory requirement of the Internal Revenue Code. However, in certain situations the IRS may forgive (abate) a penalty upon request by the taxpayer. When an assessed tax is reduced or a penalty is abated, the IRS will recompute the interest assessed to reflect the lesser amount of taxes and penalties owed to the IRS. Thus, there can be some interest savings.

There are basically two types of penalty abatements.

The "first time penalty abatement" (FTA) is an IRS administrative procedure whereby if the taxpayer qualifies, the IRS will abate certain penalties. These penalties were discussed in Chapter 2 and are the failure to file and the failure to pay. In addition, the failure to deposit penalty can also be abated. In our office, we will obtain about 20 years of transcripts for a taxpayer and review each of those years to see if a penalty was imposed on the taxpayer. After identifying the years where a penalty was assessed, we then rank the penalties in terms of penalty dollars assessed. We are most interested in the years where a significant penalty was assessed. We then analyze whether the taxpayer qualifies for the FTA. If the taxpayer qualifies, we request that the penalty be abated (forgiven) for that year.

The other penalty relief is for "reasonable cause". Many taxpayers and practitioners erroneously believe that if you state a plausible reason why the penalty should be abated, the IRS will *automatically* do so. That is not the case! Getting a penalty abated for reasonable cause is often difficult. As discussed above, the individual income tax penalties that may be abated for reasonable cause include the failure to file, the failure to pay, and the failure to deposit penalties.

Some of the more common reasons given for reasonable cause include death, serious illness, unavoidable absence, unable to obtain tax records, undue hardship, relied upon bad advice from the IRS or tax adviser, and tax records were destroyed by fire, flood or other casualty.

The IRS uses a decision support interactive software program labeled the Reasonable Cause Assistant (RCA) to reach its reasonable cause determination. This program analyzes the support provided by the taxpayer or the taxpayer's representative to support the claim for penalty relief. "Credible information" must explain the facts and circumstances showing that taxpayer *exercised ordinary business care and prudence,* and cite specific dates for the non-compliance. All information, including the dates, must substantiate why the taxpayer was unable to comply. The RCA has been programmed to include reasonable and specific time frames to allow for filing and or paying taxes after the event cited by the taxpayer preventing compliance.

The IRS typically considers four (4) criteria when deciding to abate a tax penalty for reasonable cause.

- The taxpayer needs a compelling reason for seeking relief. All appropriate explanations need to sync with the dates and circumstances on which the penalties were based.
- The IRS looks at the compliance history of the taxpayer. Bad behavior in the past may weigh negatively on the taxpayer's circumstances.
- The length of time it took the taxpayer to become compliant must be reasonable under the circumstances.
- Finally, the circumstances cited as the underlying reason for relief must be truly beyond the taxpayer's control.

Let's consider an example of a taxpayer requesting penalty abatement for reasonable cause due to a serious illness. Let's assume that the taxpayer had a major heart attack on January 1 that required a hospital stay for 45 days. During his hospital stay, he was in a coma and had to be resuscitated three times. He was released from the hospital on February 15, then spent two weeks in rehab, and returned to work on March 1. He failed to file his tax return due April 15 and cited his medical illness as reasonable cause. He eventually filed his tax return a few months after returning to work.

The IRS will very likely deny this request. Yes, the taxpayer had a compelling reason, but the dates involved with his illness do not sync with the filing due date of his return. The timing of his illness would not have prevented him from filing his return on April 15 or requesting an extension of time to file until October 15.

CHAPTER 11

Privileged Communications

Tax professionals generally have the same privilege communications with their clients that attorneys have with respect to civil matters. That privileged communication does not apply to criminal matters.

When a taxpayer is discussing their IRS tax problems with a tax professional or attorney, it is very important to show all of his cards and disclose upfront that criminal conduct may be an issue. This discussion is often referred to as an "eggshell" discussion. All parties are walking on eggshells as it is very important that all the parties understand the privileged communications rules so as not to jeopardize the taxpayer's privileged communications. Once a tax resolution specialist learns that there may be criminal activity, he needs to immediately call an attorney who specializes in IRS criminal matters and request that the attorney handle the taxpayer's tax debt case working with the tax resolution specialist through what is referred to as a "Kovel" arrangement. Using a Kovel arrangement, the attorney represents the taxpayer and the attorney engages the tax resolution specialist to handle the case for the attorney. The courts and IRS recognize that such an arrangement does not jeopardize the attorney client privilege since the accountant works for the attorney, not the taxpayer. Under such an arrangement, the accountant's work product is also privileged.

CHAPTER 12

Are You an Injured or Innocent Spouse?

The terms "injured spouse" and "innocent spouse", two entirely different solutions for resolving IRS taxes due, are often mistakenly thought by taxpayers to be the same. For purposes of this chapter as well as the previous chapters, we assume that the husband is the tax debtor and his wife is the injured or innocent spouse. A requirement for either claim is that the couple filed a joint income tax return, often referred to as married filing jointly. By filing a joint income tax return, both spouses are jointly and severally liable for the tax liability. In other words, IRS can collect its assessment of tax, interest and penalties from either spouse. Married couples have the option of filing as married filing jointly or married filing separately. Accordingly, if a spouse has a concern about any position on a return, about unreported income, questionable deductions, or the ability to full pay, consideration should be given to filing married filing separately.

While a husband and wife who file as married filing separately can later file an amended tax return and file as married filing jointly, the reverse is not true. Couples who file as married filing jointly cannot amend their filing and file as married filing separately after April 15. As you read about an innocent spouse, it is obviously why the IRS does not allow joint tax filers to be able to change to married filing separately. To do so would impair IRS collection efforts.

In community property states, married individuals face the more onerous duty to pay taxes on one-half of a spouse's income even when they file a married filing separate return.

Injured Spouse: The wife files a joint tax return with her husband and a portion or all of her expected tax refund was taken by the IRS to pay the husband's financial obligations. For example, the couple filed a joint return showing an expected refund of $1,000 but only received a refund of $200. The injured spouse learns that her husband had an outstanding student loan or an unpaid court ordered child support payment of $800. The IRS uses $800 of the $1,000 overpayment to satisfy the monies owed by the husband. The wife is injured by this action because her tax withholdings were excessive and that is why an overpayment was shown on the couple's joint tax return.

An injured spouse would file IRS Form 8379, either with the original filed return (if the husband's liability is known in advance) or after that return is filed and the wife subsequently learns that she did not receive her anticipated refund because of her husband's financial obligations. The Form 8379 requires an allocation of the income and deductions shown on the return between the two spouses. The IRS reviews this form and any supporting documentation (e.g., W-2 forms and 1099 forms that show federal tax withholdings). The IRS reviews the submitted form, makes any needed adjustments, and then will issue a refund check for the appropriate amount to the injured spouse.

Innocent Spouse: It is often said that an innocent spouse is not *that* innocent in the eyes of the IRS.

Whereas we have attempted to avoid citing the Internal Revenue Code in this book, we have made an exception in this chapter since a taxpayer can file an innocent spouse claim under IRC Secs. 6015(b), 6015(c), or 6015(f).

While not discussed in this chapter, Streamlined Innocent Spouse Relief may be available to spouses who can demonstrate that they would suffer economic hardship if relief were not granted.

Under Sec. 6015, an individual will be relieved of liability for tax (including interest and penalties) for a tax year to the extent the liability is attributable to an understatement (or tax deficiency) if the following conditions are met:

- *A joint tax return must have been filed* (Note: If one spouse asserts and establishes that he or she signed a return under legal duress, the return is not a joint return. Likewise, if one spouse did not sign the joint return, then there was not a joint return filed);
- When an innocent spouse claim is filed (again, we are assuming that the wife is the innocent spouse), the IRS will notify the husband who filed the joint return and ask if he will verify the statements of his wife seeking innocent spouse status. Imagine the response of some ex-spouses after a bitter divorce;
- There is an understatement of tax attributable to erroneous items of the non-requesting spouse (the husband);
- The requesting spouse (wife) establishes that in signing the return she did not know and had no reason to know of the item giving rise to the understatement of tax, and she may need to establish that she did not benefit from the understatement;
- It is inequitable to hold the requesting spouse (wife) liable for the deficiency attributable to the understatement caused by her husband;
- The innocent spouse files Form 8857 no later than the date that is two years (for IRC 6015(b) and 6015(c) relief) after the date the IRS has begun collection activities.

The applicable section of IRC Sec. 6015 depends upon whether the tax liability arose as a deficiency or as a filed joint return with a balance outstanding and upon the current marital status of the parties. Accordingly, let's look at the highlights of the three pertinent IRC Sec. 6015 Code sections and their similarities and differences:

Sec. 6015(b) Code section highlights:

- Provides general relief for *taxpayers who remain married;*
- Tax being assessed by the IRS is attributable to erroneous items (e.g., unreported income or incorrect deductions,

credits or tax basis) of the non-requesting spouse (or former spouse) and results from an IRS audit exam assessment (*in other words, if there is a balance due on a return filed that has not been audited by the IRS, there can be no innocent spouse claim*);

- The innocent spouse did not know <u>and</u> had no reason to know of the item giving rise to the understatement - - - *the innocent spouse has the burden of proof* and that is very difficult to prove.
- After taking into consideration all the facts and circumstances, it would be inequitable to hold the requesting spouse liable for the deficiency attributable to the understatement; and
- The claim (Form 8857) must be filed within 2 years of the date the IRS initiated its collection efforts;

IRC Sec. 6015(c) highlights:

- This is often referred to as separation of liability relief and *only applies to spouses who are either no longer married, legal separately, or were not members of the same household for the past 12 months preceding the filing of Form 8857*;
- Tax being assessed by the IRS is attributable to erroneous items (e.g., unreported income or incorrect deductions, credits or tax basis) of the non-requesting spouse (or former spouse) and results from an IRS audit exam assessment (*in other words, if there is a balance due on a return filed that has not been audited by the IRS, there can be no innocent spouse claim*);
- The innocent spouse did not know <u>and</u> had no reason to know of the item giving rise to the understatement - - - *the* **burden of proof shifts to the IRS** *in that it must prove that the electing spouse <u>knew</u> of the understatement by the other spouse to deny the claim*;
- The liability of the innocent spouse is limited to the specific liability allocable to that spouse. Thus, if all of the liability on a joint return filed prior to the divorce (or separation or living apart) related to underreported income from the

other spouse (husband), then the requesting spouse (wife) is fully relieved of liability unless the innocent spouse (wife) had knowledge of any item related to the understatement.

IRC Sec. 6015(f) highlights:

- If the taxpayer does not qualify for innocent spouse relief under Sec. 6015(b) or (c), there may be equitable relief available;
- *Relief may be granted for tax liabilities correctly reported on the return, whereas 6015(b) and (c) only grant relief for understatements (deficiencies) of tax;*
- The taxpayer is not bound by the two-year filing requirement of Form 8857, but is bound by the normal statute of limitations rules;
- In the case of *Porter v. Commissioner*, 2008, the court found that the review of such claims would be de novo - - - new evidence could be introduced by the innocent spouse;
- The taxpayer must meet a number of criteria — see IRS Revenue Procedure 2003-61 for details

CHAPTER 13

Bankruptcy

T his chapter is not a comprehensive summary of the bankruptcy law. If you are considering bankruptcy as an option to resolve your IRS tax debt, we recommend that you consult with an experienced attorney who specializes in bankruptcy law. However, we believe that a rudimentary understanding of the bankruptcy rules as they relate to the discharge of taxes is meaningful. Hopefully this chapter provides you with an overview of the basics of bankruptcy and when it may be the appropriate vehicle to solve your IRS tax problems.

Taxpayers often dismiss bankruptcy as an option to resolve their tax debts because they don't want to ruin their credit. What many of these taxpayers don't realize is that by having IRS liens and levies filed against them, their credit is already in the proverbial toilet. Accordingly, bankruptcy should not be automatically dismissed as it may be the taxpayer's best option to solve their IRS tax debt problem.

One of the fundamental goals of the federal bankruptcy law is to give debtors a "fresh start" from their overwhelming debts. Unfortunately, there are individuals and attorneys who mistakenly believe that income taxes cannot be discharged in bankruptcy. Likewise, there are individuals who mistakenly believe that by declaring bankruptcy, all their IRS tax debt is forgiven. Before dismissing bankruptcy as a tax resolution option, or when bankruptcy is being considered as an option, an experienced attorney who specializes in bankruptcy law needs to be consulted and should work closely with a tax resolution specialist. While an attorney may specialize in bankruptcy law, he or she may not be familiar with the Internal Revenue Code as it pertains to IRS tax debts. The date that a taxpayer files for bankruptcy can have a VERY profound effect and possibly result in certain taxes not being eligible for discharge. If you are interviewing a bankruptcy attorney, be sure to ask if s/he works with a tax resolution specialist.

The three most common types of bankruptcies for resolving tax debts are Chapter 7, Chapter 11 and Chapter 13 (for individual wage earners).

The goal of Chapter 7 is to discharge debt, providing the debtor with a fresh start. The bankruptcy trustee will liquidate nonexempt assets (a bankruptcy term) to pay the debtors. Chapter 7 allows the debtor to be relieved of all debt that is dischargeable. The general rule is that income taxes are not dischargeable unless they fall into one of the three fundamental rules stated below. In addition to having income taxes discharged, it may be possible to have IRS interest and penalties discharged. When filing a Chapter 7 bankruptcy, the interest and penalties follow the taxes. If the income tax is found dischargeable, then so are the interest and penalties. Likewise, if the income tax is not dischargeable in a Chapter 7 filing, then the interest and penalties will survive the bankruptcy.

Chapter 11 and Chapter 13 bankruptcy filings are similar to a repayment plan where the debt is restructured and paid back. Although available to individuals, Chapter 11 is usually used by corporations as individuals find Chapter 13 more advantageous because of its simplicity, it's less costly, and has broader discharge provisions. The debtor gets to keep his assets, and the bankruptcy court grants time to repay the creditors, sometimes without interest. While interest continues to accrue under a Chapter 11 filing, it does not under Chapter 13. Penalties over three years old may be dischargeable.

There are three fundamental rules to determine whether an income tax is dischargeable in bankruptcy. These rules are referred to as the 3-year rule, the 2-year rule, and the 240-day rule.

The 3-year rule means that the *tax has to be 3-years old.* In other words, 3 years must have passed since the income tax return was due (including extensions) and the bankruptcy filing date. For example, a 2012 return filed on April 15, 2013 would satisfy the 3-year rule once three years have passed. In this case, April 15, 2016 would satisfy the 3-year rule. It is important that the taxpayer actually filed a tax return. *If the IRS prepared a substitute for return (SFR), the tax for that year is not dischargeable even when the taxpayer later files a return.*

The 2-year rule means that in addition to meeting the 3-year rule, the tax return must have been filed at least two years prior to the date of the bankruptcy filing. This rule is commonly applicable when tax returns are filed late. Let's assume that a return was due on April 15, 2015, was granted an extension of time to file until October 15, 2015, but that the return was not filed until October 22, 2015. To meet the 2-year rule, the bankruptcy filing date could not be before October 22, 2017.

The 240-day rule means that if there was any assessment, including additional assessments, those assessments must be 240-days old. An additional assessment could arise as a result of an IRS audit examination.

If all three of these criteria are met, then that income tax is dischargeable in bankruptcy. There are exceptions. For example, taxes due to the filing of a fraudulent return or because of tax evasion are not dischargeable. Keep in mind that we are addressing income taxes being discharged in bankruptcy. Payroll and withholding taxes (including trust fund taxes), real estate and property taxes, and excise taxes are not dischargeable.

When a taxpayer files for bankruptcy, generally all IRS collection efforts cease immediately. The SOL is suspended during the filing of the bankruptcy plus six (6) months.

Types of Tax Claims include pre-petition and post-petition claims. We will focus on the pre-petition claims. These are income taxes that relate to a tax year that ends before the date that bankruptcy is filed. Pre-petition tax claims are further designated as secured or unsecured, with the unsecured claims further divided into priority or general unsecured claims.

The IRS has a secured claim (taxes, interest and penalties) if a Notice of Federal Tax Lien was filed and to the extent there is equity in the taxpayer's property. If a Notice of Federal Tax Lien was not filed or there is no equity in the taxpayer's property, the claim is unsecured. Thus if a Notice of Federal Tax Lien was filed and there is only enough equity in the property to cover a portion of the IRS's claim, then the IRS has a secured claim to the extent there is equity and an unsecured claim for the balance.

If the 3-year, 2-year, and the 240-day rules are not satisfied, the IRS has a priority claim against the taxpayer. Priority taxes cannot be discharged in bankruptcy. If these three tests are satisfied by the taxpayer, the IRS has a non-priority claim.

In summary, priority claims are not good for tax resolution purposes. Income taxes that are dischargeable in bankruptcy are unsecured and are not a priority claim.

CHAPTER 14

Summary

We hope that the taxpayers who read this book will obtain a better understanding of the complex IRS collections process and the different payment options that may be available to them dependent upon their individual circumstances and the facts of their case.

We encourage our readers to begin to address their IRS tax problems immediately by consulting with a tax resolution specialist when the first IRS notice is received, or better yet, when the tax return is filed showing a balance due that cannot be immediately paid.

Remember that it is always better to file a tax return showing a balance due without the accompanying tax remittance, rather than not filing a tax return because you cannot afford to pay the taxes due. The former subjects you to the failure to pay penalty, whereas the latter course of action subjects you to both the failure to file and failure to pay penalty.

When the IRS accepts you in a payment program, you need to make sure that if you are a W-2 employee that sufficient federal withholdings are made from your pay, and if you are self-employed, that you are paying an adequate amount of estimated taxes each quarter. You also need to file all tax returns on time. If you are found to be non-compliant, the hard work in reaching an installment agreement or OIC with the IRS will be for naught and you will find yourself again in collections with the IRS hounding you for payment.

If you owe the IRS less than $10,000, you may be able to handle resolving your IRS tax debt yourself. It would be beneficial to you to first speak with a tax resolution specialist before attempting to resolve your tax debt. Naturally, as your tax debt grows in terms of dollars and the number of tax years involved increase, you will usually find that hiring a tax resolution specialist is your best course of action. In most cases, the potential tax savings (including interest and penalties) and peace of mind using a tax resolution specialist's expertise and experience will more than pay for those services.

Where do you find an experienced and knowledgeable tax resolution specialist? We suggest you visit the American Society of Tax Problem Solvers website (www.astps.org) which is a non-profit organization that monitors its members to ensure that they operate ethically and have the proper training and where you will find we are members in good standing.

If you wish to contact us for a free consultation, you can call us at (610) 594-2601 or visit our website, www.stopmytaxproblems.com.